Daily Blessings

Poems on Tractate Berakhot

Hillel Broder

Ben Yehuda Press
Teaneck, New Jersey

Published by Ben Yehuda Press
122 Ayers Court #1B
Teaneck, NJ 07666

http://www.BenYehudaPress.com

Jewish Poetry Project #25
http://jpoetry.us

To subscribe to our monthly book club and support independent Jewish publishing, visit https://www.patreon.com/BenYehudaPress

ISBN13 978-1-953829-30-6

Library of Congress Cataloging-in-Publication Data

Names: Broder, Hillel, author.
Title: Daily blessings : poems on tractate Berakhot / Hillel Broder.
Description: Teaneck, New Jersey : Ben Yehuda Press, [2022] | Series:
  Jewish poetry project ; 25 | Summary: "Poems responding to each page of
  Tractate Berakhot of the Babylonian Talmud"-- Provided by publisher.
Identifiers: LCCN 2022024691 | ISBN 9781953829306 (paperback)
Subjects: LCGFT: Poetry.
Classification: LCC PS3602.R63448 D35 2022 | DDC 811/.6--dc23/
eng/20220527
LC record available at https://lccn.loc.gov/2022024691

22 23 24 / 10 9 8 7 6 5 4 3 2 1   20220715

DEDICATION

For my father,
who is my *daf yomi* pioneer,
and who taught and teaches us what's possible
through discipline, hard work,
and daily study.

CONTENTS

ACKNOWLEDGMENTS

First, a very special thank you to my wife, Eva, for wholeheartedly supporting this and all of our projects. What's mine is yours.

And thank you to all who believed in and read selections of this work publicly on Twitter, as part of a private Facebook writing group, or on various WhatsApp chats. This work was conceived digitally, and friends and colleagues reading through these various social media offered useful feedback on content and form, encouraging it towards completion and publication.

PREFACE

For almost 100 years, Jews around the world have studied the vast sea of the Talmud on a *daf yomi* calendar, a page scheduled for each day. This modern movement has both united and popularized Talmud study well beyond the walls and years of the traditional yeshiva and academy. At this rate, the Talmud's full study of its nearly 3,000 pages is completed every 7.5 years or so.

With the celebration in January 2020 of the completion of a full cycle and the start of a new cycle, this book was initiated as a personal challenge to follow and continue the daily study with a poetic response.

As the Talmud begins with *Masechet Brachot*, the tractate concerned most with prayer, blessings, and Jewish law as it relates to daily living, I found that it naturally offered wisdom, law, and teachings that might be focused in verse. I also found that sharing each poem with a daily writing group allowed me to experiment with different forms of poetic response. You'll notice that I favored a more condensed format as the poems evolve.

Of course, the Talmud's pages are arbitrarily designated—their starts and ends are the result of histories of printing presses. What emerged for me, then, was both a necessarily creative selection and synthesis in focusing on the language and rhythms of the page, as

Hillel Broder

well as an eye for thematic development across pages, too. I was particularly interested in how disparate elements seemed to respond to one another.

This book was not written or composed for any particular audience. It was my accountability project, my daily assignment, response, and checkpoint following the daily page's study. For others, it might serve as a standalone work, or as a companion for those embarking on the daily study of this tractate.

Ultimately, my hope is that it inspires others to see and hear the verse in the Talmud's pages—as the Talmud is neither novel or newspaper, neither textbook or law book. It is, instead, written in the rhythms of spoken word, describing and prescribing lived experience through a living language.

CHAPTER 1:
FROM WHEN?

Berakhot 2

what exactly
was our point of departure
for starting with the evening,

so that we begin
with begging its question.

plenty occurs
when it's time to recline:

sunsets, in other words,
are inevitable,
and the first day, on the eve of creation,
started with a sunset, but also

purified priests enter the Temple,
poor man's bread is dipped in salt,
and the Sabbath is sanctified.

ultimately, everything rises
until sunrise, say the Sages,
but we need to start somewhere,

and if we ended
at the end, well, then,
we would, no doubt,
be far too close to sin.

Hillel Broder

Berakhot 3

heaven's roars echo in ruins
muted, like pigeons cooing,
like housewives whispering
to nurslings and husbands:
I am walking in the dark, alone
and with Elijah, I am praying
that the roof not collapse, that I not
be suspect, that the demons avoid me,
and it is already late enough, and
the time has arrived
to read the Sh'ma.

a wind has stirred my harp,
and at once we are not alone in our houses
of study and song, as ruinous
and as ready to collapse
they might be.

Berakhot 4

on the tenth of Tevet,
I saw the day's aging prayers
on the daily page:

sin brought redemption
in natural guises;

humiliation of David
and his nation wrought
greatness; in exile,
I read, it is best to link
redemption to prayer,
so that prayer
becomes redemption,

to order one's prayers,
in other words,
alphabetically, so that nothing falls
through the indeterminate crack
of midnight, into the haziness
of praying the evening service
at all. it's messy, yes, as a king
distinguishes various bloods
from afterbirths:

and for that,
we are pious and pray
that we won't be obliged
to give our lives.

Hillel Broder

Berakhot 5

death is the ultimate motivator,
but suffering begs the question.

when you lie down, you might do so
with a double-edged sword
as if on your deathbed
or the small bone of a child's hand,
a shard of suffering
cleansing the body,
like a damaged slave, now free
to say: woe to the hurt and its reward!

and when you rise, you do so
as a prisoner set free
by another's hand, you do so by
a divine gift economy—
God's gift is His gain, and ours, too;

and when you depart,
you cry over a friend's beauty
and its inevitable decay.

in affliction we are
alone: words, places
and worlds to come.

Berakhot 6

He's ready:

just sing, and you're praying;
just assemble, He's waiting;
just judge, He'll join;

just study, together or
alone, He's holding
the space between the eye
and text, somewhere
amidst demons
best not seen;

there's a box bound to his mind:
He's devoted His will
and chosen you.

most of the time,
the work's not the point:
He's just there, already
waiting for you
to rise and take
your usual place,

to run, crowd, or pontificate
even if you can't make out
the words or truth. The main thing
to be sure, on your way:
greet Him and all Others.

offer and take,
exchange Peace.

Hillel Broder

Berakhot 7

because we don't contain
our voices and prayers
our wills and intentions:

our house of prayer is God's house
for prayer, like a river pouring
out and into itself,
like flower petals
unfolding into our words.

our actions, their effects:
because habits
of generations still hum
just beneath the surface,
it is impossible to guess
the moment
when anger rises and passes.

Berakhot 8

we are full of whole and broken
minds and hearts,
and because
we are lives who find
either suffering or delight, who
are extracted in death
roughly or with ease,
who derive pleasure
from our own hands' labor,
we all end up in the same place
in this world.

it is best to store and stage everyone
in the same place
in the next: tucked away
in the same box,
or somewhere out there,
in a field,
since the walls have ears,
and in plain sight.

study alone, but when we read,
together; go early or go late
to our gathering house—
just be a good neighbor.

Hillel Broder

Berakhot 9

words take on double meaning
when the human leaves and
reaches towards divine and time
turns elastic: hurry, in haste,
both Israel and Egypt,
so that the time of redemption
and its sacrificial lamb
starts and ends
both in the evening
and the morning,
so that a plunderer's
exit is both a gift and
in its delay a burden.

the difference is as narrow
as redemption
and the prayer that accompanies it,

as the moment you know
the difference between a donkey
and a wild donkey—
that's when
the ancient ones taught us
would be ideal
to welcome the day
and recognize
a good friend.

Berakhot 10

I contain and create
worlds of
form within form,
shaped and singing
within my womb, to my breasts,
towards the stars,
onto death;

milk's kindness emanates
from my heart—

love sinners,
pray for their sins:
if your enemies are
just bandits, will them
to return and repent.

and my host wisdom
of soup, sheets,
attics, and walls:
who you invoke,
your lowest places,
tells me everything
I need to know.

Hillel Broder

Berakhot 11

rise and be seated
rest and walk;
with only one
great love

on your mind,
you see how
with a great love
one contains the other:
the night mentions
the day, darkness
recalls light,

though we can't recall
which was said
before each priestly watch
and after every study session:

with a great love

you might as well
bless them all.

Berakhot 12

so much more was heard at Sinai
than the ten commandments.

lest those who know mislead or
trick those who don't,
we didn't include it.

on the other hand, on the Sabbath
we add a new blessing
offered in the Temple
from the outgoing
to the incoming watch:

the One whose Name
dwells in this House—
may He cause to dwell
among you: a great love,
harmony, peace
and friendship.

everything goes after the blessing's
end, and so even as we don't mention
God's name in its opening or
His kingdom in its closing,

the day contains the night's faith,
and the night contains the day's thanks,
and the opening blessing,
even if said in error,
contains both
name and kingdom.

Hillel Broder

Bending when we bless, straightening
at the Name—

we are always already
bent straight, like a stick; and since
The Name straightens the crooked:

raise your head, and then each
vertebra, proud like a snake, rises.

Berakhot 13

the point: the heart should listen
for a moment
to its own language;
leaving Egypt
is a brief interruption,
a hand passing over eyes
in a study hall.

and in a moment,
it is forgotten
not from memory, but
from the body
because an exponential
regression of wolves,
lions, snakes,
happens in a moment
again and again.

remember your body's
history, but also remember
that as you are interrupted
by fear and peace,
traumas displace
your name by others and
your names break
open into histories,

so that for a long moment
you are not only a
father, but the father
and mother of worlds

Hillel Broder

in all four directions
birthing listening hearts,
wrestling with God.

Hillel Broder

CHAPTER 2:
HE WAS READING

Berakhot 14

learn, to teach,
teach, to create:
with double truths
of authority and action,
little precedes the other,

just like dream logic,
a taste can't satiate, so
beware of confusing
the two.

it is as if you testified
falsely or built an altar
outside of the temple

it is like dreamless sleep
for seven days:

you are too satiated
to taste.

Hillel Broder

Berakhot 15

if cries emerge from the womb,
how much more so
will cries emerge
from the grave:
both are never filled
to capacity
by words, whispered
or shouted, and so
somewhere between thoughts
uttered by the heart
and words heard by the ear

is the difference between hell,
when cries overwhelm
their words, and a cooler hell,
when words are split apart
by their sounds.

This is a proof for those who doubt
a Biblical source
for the return of the dead.

Berakhot 16

because our forefathers
were born of servant
foremothers, and because the
beloved servants of the Talmud
were called father and mother,

we invoke all of our foremothers
in their absence, the same singular
quiet that fills a loss
or that follows a wandering mind
away from the intention
to hear that which is spoken
by the heart at every moment:

like one whose work is in trees,
whose ship has sunk, whose thoughts
are elsewhere with the task at hand:
a fresh union.

one is reminded of the rabbi who retreats
from his students
as they pursue him
into inner corridors
upon the loss of his servant:

inconsolable, without a ritual,
waiting to return, in silence.

Hillel Broder

Berakhot 17

my God: before creation,
I was nothing,
and now
I'm useless. Even more so
in my death.

at the very least,
make my soul like dust
to others,
so that in the end,
some good name remains.

may it be, today
and every day, to receive
a good friend to see our faults—
may they be as great and as few
as our ancestors' sins.

save us from anger,
ours and yours,
and harmonize
upper and lower worlds
noble and practical
useless and useful.

may it be your will
that my desire becomes
the desire—

that is my only will, only that
a slight fermenting
gets in the way

may its fat dissolve
in today's suffering and
become my offering.

may it be one desire:
the words of my mouth
the thoughts of my heart—

heard and seen
before you and me.

CHAPTER 3:
ONE WHOSE DEAD

Berakhot 18

because the living know that
bodies are hidden

just beneath the tips
of their fringes,
like orphans' charity,
stowed away
in the maws of earth,

in another room or
just behind the curtain;

in the bones of a saddlebag
or with us, in our very boat;

the living know that
as children of life
they have already died.

the living dead,
however, know nothing
and so are already dead.

and as
we don't know if the dead,
after their deaths,
know or care of our matters,

even as they converse
with one another, listen
to the stories
of ghosts: my friend,

my friend, it is the eve
of judgment, let us go and roam
through the world, eavesdrop
beyond the curtain
about the world and its
coming retributions.

but be careful:
the matters between us
have and will be heard
among the living.

Berakhot 19

it is forbidden to speak of
or for the dead, and yet we must
leap over coffins, repair the breaches,
and dignify bodies, even if we hide
and contaminate ourselves,
and sit, do nothing and recite
just a verse, even if wisdom and Satan
are given voice.

Hillel Broder

Berakhot 20

as prayer is the soul's
constant activity
and brought by time's
mimicry within cycles
of travel, meals, study:
beneath it all,
there is an acceptance
of eternity,

always home, like fish
hidden beneath the sea—

always a raised head
at every doorway.

Berakhot 21

if only one might pray all day,
and because we do,
and because
we were at Sinai
but also too impure to
learn, we forgot if
and when we pray.
there's hope when
others challenge us
to join them, and
when fathers teach sons—
then, we return to Sinai,
then, we make it new.

Berakhot 22

because the Torah was given
in fire, it once happened
that an impure student trembled
before his teacher who said
my son, open your mouth
and let your words spill
as words of Torah
like fire, illuminate, and therefore
never become impure.

Berakhot 23

because our pores and needs
will betray us even as we
prepare ourselves
and guard our feet
to greet our God, we keep
reminders close, but not too
close—we can forget them, too,
when we fail to distinguish
between good
and its opposite, when we
sin knowing that we can repent.

Hillel Broder

Berakhot 24

one who raises his voice
is of little faith, unless
his heart can't hear
his own whispers:

like an unseen sneeze,
a pleasure below, then above;
like lying unclothed,
we turn away,
or turn to the other,
bodies brushing,
flatly squatting,
blessed cavities—

Master of the Universe—

destined for worms.

Berakhot 25

we are not angels, after all,
and so not all of our prayers
are to God, some are reminders
that our mouths can praise
apart from our limbs, which all
sing praises, even when soiled;
that excrement eventually crumbles,
that urine runs and dries,
that men and pigs
both defecate,
out of both mouths;

that our hearts
and our other parts can
sink into a murky sty
and not be seen
by their own nakedness.

Hillel Broder

CHAPTER 4:
THE PRAYER OF DAWN

Berakhot 26

as our fathers
rose to dawn
and spoke in fields
to meet the place
of crooked time,
we bring day
into night:
passing time
with prayer—
an imperfect sacrifice.

Hillel Broder

Berakhot 27

in a sky gathering with clouds
the night brings permission
to be endless—burn fats,
whenever, and when the clouds
scatter and the sun shines,
we wonder about time passing
when it didn't, so did we
ever pray?

an answer: prayer is prayer,
and gatherings of clouds
can't be bothered by time.

Berakhot 28

at night, some stand still, lock the doors,
lead the few obliged to pray.
others know that the pallor outside
is the same as your inner, filthy walls,
a preoccupation enough to stay silent

and say: you can't argue with the living,
they are like beards that brighten overnight,

and while every beautiful glass eventually breaks,
it's better to seize it, and anything is possible.

this is the secret of leading
through the night:
we beg its question
to show its splendor.

Hillel Broder

Berakhot 29

the spine holds burdens.
extend each vertebra
like the voices of the sea
the joy of inauguration
the rays of the sun—
just make it new, so that on
the road, passing by bandits,
you might mutter: insight us
to know your ways; what's best
in your eyes, do unto us.

Hillel Broder

CHAPTER 5:
WE DON'T STAND

Berakhot 30

the ancient ones would
wait for a moment
until full or empty,
and with a head's heaviness
turn hearts towards the tower
of a neck adorned by
open mouths, a center
from every direction,

just like the blind, who stop
on the way,
and turn towards heaven,
and the goodness
of a friend.

Hillel Broder

Berakhot 31

let me rise to prayer
out of joy—
as a drunk,
fill my mouth
with laughter,
direct my heart
to the heavens,
so that if you leave me
in one corner,
like a beggar,
you'll find me
in another.

let my mouth
cut my words
and throw them
upward:

give me a son
to nurse
from my heart.

Berakhot 32

the lion only roars when full.
only when words
fail, when sick
with bones on fire,
when hope after
follows hope before,
and you throw everything
upward—then the matter depends
on you alone.

happy is the student
whose teacher agrees
to forget—
and receives life.

Hillel Broder

Berakhot 33

You have made known to us
the differences between
the ends of Yourself,
circles within circles,
a Temple of the mind,
sanctified, like a snake bite
of the sinless, so that rain
contains the revival
of the dead.

Berakhot 34

peasants nod, while kings
bow for days. awe is a small thing
for the few—are the heavens a friend?
are there beggars forever?

no eye has seen its reward.
if your words flow, if you
salt yourself, perfectly:

refuse, then stretch
out your legs, and pass
before the ark.

Hillel Broder

CHAPTER 6:
HOW DO WE BLESS?

Berakhot 35

until Elijah arrives,
your mind is everyone's:
let your wine sing, your bread fill.

plow when you plow; in the way of the land,
gather your grain. God has set the table,
and you will return the blessing to Father
and Mother. taste the world, and remember
the first ones: what will become of their Torah?

remove the table: it's yours.

Hillel Broder

Berakhot 36

a tree whose words for wood and fruit
are no different in taste:
between primary and secondary
healing and pleasure
grounded and flowering
shell, bud, and crown.
first in Eden, now a peppercorn tree:
a reminder and harbinger
that the land of Israel
lacks nothing.

Berakhot 37

because the flow of the land
satisfies as much as grains
nourish, some thank God
fully, for the good land fills.

others condense their blessings,
jumping with the majority; they
thank for the array of excess,
and are renewed in a Temple
of bread crumbs.

Berakhot 38

as poor man's bread,
we were taken
from the ground, misted
from a date, boiled
from a rock.

others say we are still
extracting, by
drinking Egyptian
beer on Shabbat—

bitter exile
healing exodus still—

like a master, still
removing himself
from dispute.

Berakhot 39

Solomon's peace for the broken:

you can't choose a blessing over a beloved.
fold fragments within the whole, conclude
with a cut, and complete them together.

they will be as olives without pits: stores
of aged wisdom doubling a pauper's bread
at a shared meal.

Hillel Broder

Berakhot 40

before you eat the compassionate bread
of Eden, feed its master's knowledge
to another, even a small fish;

it will multiply you like a tree,
whose branches remain again
and fill you when you, the old fruit,
make it new, giving each day
its own blessing,
in its own language.

Berakhot 41

when blessings seem the same
what you choose
is not the closest choice,
which for some, like
a bronze foundation,
is the measuring stick
of the world.

a closely held olive
serves a radish
in silence, like a loaf
smothering its
dishes and dips.

Hillel Broder

Berakhot 42

wisdom's students are blessed guests:
meals continue to usher bread
beyond dessert; wine is timeless like
a bathhouse or the sabbath; redeemed,
prayer is ready, a sacrifice waiting
to be offered. otherwise: we are torn
on both sides, interrupted on our
way; we are no longer free
to recline together.

Berakhot 43

scholars are fragrant alone,
a subtle scent,
as myrtle without oil—
instead of burning
in others, their work
is enough in their own eyes;
bringing souls to sing.
they remember to take care
of their shoes, to walk bent
and quiet, whitening faces
by the moon.

Hillel Broder

Berakhot 44

go out and see:
though sweet needs salty,
we only bless the sweet.
though throats are first
to slaughter, we bless them
for their proximity to life.
though diminutives diminish,
a full sardine restores the soul.
while foods demand it,
actions and smells don't
close in blessing.

Hillel Broder

CHAPTER 7:
THREE THAT EAT

Berakhot 45

three exalting as one is an invitation
to call in response,
and even from the market,
and only in translation
by my voice, which I will decrease,
to match yours, so that
when we are great, we are together.
listen: I will yell and whisper amen
to end my own blessing

Berakhot 46

good is hidden in the breach
of truth, a host's loaf
broken by a generous eye
in a house
of mourning;
and a guest blessing
a host: may your hands
work without Satan
and sin; may they stay
close to home; may the good
and truthful Judge allow nothing
to stand before
or between us.

Berakhot 47

honor is adopted on the threshold,
waiting for the other
to break bread first
between a blessing
and its extended response,
or the greatest yet to arrive.

honor is an invitation
to the convert to join,
to the plant to take root.

to the hope that a child will flourish,
a slave, freed,

that even the ark will join in,
for the sake of us all.

Berakhot 48

on the good mountain
young gourds sprout
towards roofs and heavens

with bread before them
they bless their hunger,
with the moment's end

they sit between kings and queens
holding wine
and the honor of the good
and bless the world to come.

their eternity rests between
comforts
offered in exiles.

Berakhot 49

because we don't bundle blessings
we bless land
that produces fruit;
we sanctify selves
that sanctify time;
we eat an olive, and filled
by an egg, we thank
the One who sits
upon the cherubs.

with or without eating,
erring in memory,
we can still thank
for the gifts of love:
rest, memory, joy.

Berakhot 50

respect bread
water wine,
waiters stumble between,
but eat from your own loaf:

sit together,
but don't eat,
but don't remove yourself—

even the fetus
in the womb
at the splitting
of the sea
sings of, lives by,
eats from
the good
alone.

Berakhot 51

lest the angel of death
dance before you:
without the left,
hold the right;
without another,
wash, dress yourself;
boundless together
raise your hands
take a cup
full of love:
it will hold
the sea and the south
this world
and the next—
and pass it on:
blessed be the fruit.

Hillel Broder

CHAPTER 8:
THESE ARE THE MATTERS

Berakhot 52

the whole world agrees
that a light was created after the Sabbath
on the eve of creation. for some,
it is still created, like wine occasioning
the day, darkness creating light,
or mountains reaching heavens,
a frequency so constant,
its echoes still ripple—
even if we can't heed them—
in red, white, and green.

Berakhot 53

just as a dove is only saved
by its wings, fly back
to the Temple Mount,
seek out its golden light,
even from afar,
for while in truth you may bless
wherever you are, the mighty
interrupt their studies
to call in response, imagining
golden purses digested
only to descend and discover
yourself
as a golden dove.

Hillel Broder

CHAPTER 9:
THE ONE WHO SEES

Berakhot 54

for God's wonders
we are grateful:
for mountains that cling,
and for giants that fall,
for walls swallowed,
and for judgments
of salt, for the seas
and for those
who descend to sea,
wander in wilderness,
and sit in darkness, alone
and walk free—
blessed is the One
who has granted us
more of a good life.

Hillel Broder

Berakhot 55

a dreamer's residue is strewn
upon his table
like bitter water waiting
for priests to spread hands
and make peace
of a temple's dream
of vessels, a dream opened
inside a dream, wisdom
for the wise outliving its dreamer,
like an elephant imagined
in the eye of a needle—
in the shadow of God.

Berakhot 56

I see a dream:
my nose cuts off,
I split in half,
my brains spill out.

before the words in your mouth
double my thoughts,
arise: anger falls away,
like a pillow feather,
spreading wisdom widely.

better that my wife's family
is a foreign nation, than I see
my own two eyes, kissing,
like olives in their own oil.

Berakhot 57

the new life of dreams, like the sun,
is a taste of another world,
when you wake with prophecy
tumbling out of your mouth,
recalling such unrestricted
defecation. you were nude
with a goose, taking wisdom
betrothed—then, seeing a broken
glass, you know that your dream
was already granted.

Berakhot 58

being a good guest in this world
is knowing that what is grown
and sewn for everyone was waiting
for your arrival, a blinding silence
after a storm; for the secret of your
face to emerge, like a hand,
hidden by others' charity to honor you
with wisdom apportioned
and springing from above,
returning us both to life.

Hillel Broder

Berakhot 59

creation's clean sky
first lost two stars
and is now filled by
two tears, dropping one
at a time, quaking like hands
shaking, a blessed goodness,
but only when shared, like a groom
falling on his face
filling his pit with his own dirt
at the sight of his bride:
a rainbow.

Berakhot 60

permission's power is strongest, so sit up,
stand, take a step—even if a cry
has already been heard, a fetus already
conceived, have faith, perhaps it is a rumor,
perhaps seeds were sown together—your rooster
is still calling, your candle hasn't gone out
yet, it's still early enough to pray:

all that is done with compassion
is done with goodness; for both
the giving and the taking
we will sing.

Berakhot 61

like a fox tempting fish to flee,
walking behind our backs
raises a first thought: two should
have been one, like fish in water—
a unity extended, until their souls
are taken. now, following our own tails,
as flies or kernels of wheat, we build
our storehouse, braiding our bread.

Berakhot 62

even if it is not the way of the land
I will follow you to your toilet, to your
laughter's needs, hearing how you are

as if you had never tasted
before, for you are Torah,
and its study I need.

because being alone
is the greatest test of your modesty—

it can breed demons like goats;
it can be the silence
that ends your suffering
by being seen
in the Temple,

the pupil of Your eye.

Hillel Broder

Berakhot 63

in a time to act for God
violate His Torah, know Him,
even in sin; even if you
climb a mountain, build an altar,
play a flute, like a fool,
and renounce your part.

offer a response
for every blessing: gathering in,
spread out, to gather in;

in a place where there is
a man, there—do not be a man,

silence your selves, and let it be
like the day it was given at Sinai.

Berakhot 64

if you wait,
time pushes you forward,

better to be the mountain
than the grinder of mountains,
but your time is all the same—

better to go to peace than depart
in peace, but even the righteous are restless
in the next world, building from strength
to strength, speaking peace

for the sake of their brothers
and the house of God.

Hillel Broder

ABOUT THE AUTHOR

Hillel Broder earned a Ph.D. in English from the Graduate Center of the City University of New York.

He currently serves as Principal at DRS Yeshiva High School for Boys of the Hebrew Academy of Long Beach.

Hillel Broder's first book of poems, Counting Spheres & other poems (2017), is a kabbalistic experiment in verse. This is his second book of poetry.

Comments can be directed to hbroder@gmail.com.

Hillel Broder

The Jewish Poetry Project

jpoetry.us

BenYehuda Press

From the Coffee House of Jewish Dreamers: Poems of Wonder and Wandering and the Weekly Torah Portion by Isidore Century

"Isidore Century is a wonderful poet. His poems are funny, deeply observed, without pretension." – *The Jewish Week*

The House at the Center of the World: Poetic Midrash on Sacred Space by Abe Mezrich

"Direct and accessible, Mezrich's midrashic poems often tease profound meaning out of his chosen Torah texts. These poems remind us that our Creator is forgiving, that the spiritual and physical can inform one another, and that the supernatural can be carried into the everyday."
—Yehoshua November, author of *God's Optimism*

we who desire: Poems and Torah riffs by Sue Swartz

"Sue Swartz does magnificent acrobatics with the Torah. She takes the English that's become staid and boring, and adds something that's new and strange and exciting. These are poems that leave a taste in your mouth, and you walk away from them thinking, what did I just read? Oh, yeah. It's the Bible."
—Matthue Roth, author, *Yom Kippur A Go-Go*

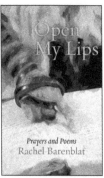

Open My Lips: Prayers and Poems
by Rachel Barenblat

"Barenblat's God is a personal God—one who lets her cry on His shoulder, and who rocks her like a colicky baby. These poems bridge the gap between the ineffable and the human. This collection will bring comfort to those with a religion of their own, as well as those seeking a relationship with some kind of higher power."
—Satya Robyn, author, *The Most Beautiful Thing*

Words for Blessing the World: Poems in Hebrew and English by Herbert J. Levine

"These writings express a profoundly earth-based theology in a language that is clear and comprehensible. These are works to study and learn from."
—Rodger Kamenetz, author, *The Jew in the Lotus*

Shiva Moon: Poems by Maxine Silverman

"The poems, deeply felt, are spare, spoken in a quiet but compelling voice, as if we were listening in to her inner life. This book is a precious record of the transformation saying Kaddish can bring."
—Howard Schwartz, author, *The Library of Dreams*

is: heretical Jewish blessings and poems
by Yaakov Moshe (Jay Michaelson)

"Finally, Torah that speaks to and through the lives we are actually living: expanding the tent of holiness to embrace what has been cast out, elevating what has been kept down, advancing what has been held back, reveling in questions, revealing contradictions."
—Eden Pearlstein, aka eprhyme

Texts to the Holy: Poems
by Rachel Barenblat

"These poems are remarkable, radiating a love of God that is full bodied, innocent, raw, pulsating, hot, drunk. I can hardly fathom their faith but am grateful for the vistas they open. I will sit with them, and invite you to do the same."
—Merle Feld, author of *A Spiritual Life*

The Sabbath Bee: Love Songs to Shabbat
by Wilhelmina Gottschalk

"Torah, say our sages, has seventy faces. As these prose poems reveal, so too does Shabbat. Here we meet Shabbat as familiar housemate, as the child whose presence transforms a family, as a spreading tree, as an annoying friend who insists on being celebrated, as a woman, as a man, as a bee, as the ocean."
—Rachel Barenblat, author, *The Velveteen Rabbi's Haggadah*

All the Holes Line Up: Poems and Translations
by Zackary Sholem Berger

"Spare and precise, Berger's poems gaze unflinchingly at—but also celebrate—human imperfection in its many forms. And what a delight that Berger also includes in this collection a handful of his resonant translations of some of the great Yiddish poets." —Yehoshua November, author of *God's Optimism* and *Two World Exist*

How to Bless the New Moon: The Priestess Paths Cycle and Other Poems for Queens
by Rachel Kann

"To read Rachel Kann's poems is to be confronted with the possibility that you, too, are prophet and beloved, touched by forces far beyond your mundane knowing. So, dear reader, enter into the 'perfumed forcefield' of these words—they are healing and transformative."
—Rabbi Jill Hammer, co-author of *The Hebrew Priestess*

Into My Garden
by David Caplan

"The beauty of Caplan's book is that it is not polemical. It does not set out to win an argument or ask you whether you've put your tefillin on today. These gentle poems invite the reader into one person's profound, ambiguous religious experience."
—*The Jewish Review of Books*

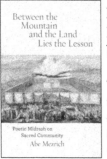

Between the Mountain and the Land is the Lesson: Poetic Midrash on Sacred Community
by Abe Mezrich

"Abe Mezrich cuts straight back to the roots of the Midrashic tradition, sermonizing as a poet, rather than idealogue. Best of all, Abe knows how to ask questions and avoid the obvious answers."
—Jake Marmer, author, *Jazz Talmud*

NOKADDISH: Poems in the Void
by Hanoch Guy Kaner

"A subversive, midrashic play with meanings—specifically Jewish meanings, and then the reversal and negation of these meanings."
—Robert G. Margolis

An Added Soul: Poems for a New Old Religion
by Herbert Levine

"These poems are remarkable, radiating a love of God that is full bodied, innocent, raw, pulsating, hot, drunk. I can hardly fathom their faith but am grateful for the vistas they open. I will sit with them, and invite you to do the same."
—Merle Feld, author of *A Spiritual Life*.

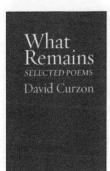

What Remains
by David Curzon

"Aphoristic, ekphrastic, and precise revelations animate WHAT REMAINS. In his stunning rewriting of Psalm 1 and other biblical passages, Curzon shows himself to be a fabricator, a collector, and an heir to the literature, arts, and wisdom traditions of the planet."
—Alicia Ostriker, author of *The Volcano and After*

The Shortest Skirt in Shul
by Sass Oron

"These poems exuberantly explore gender, Torah, the masks we wear, and the way our bodies (and the ways we wear them) at once threaten stable narratives, and offer the kind of liberation that saves our lives."
—Alicia Jo Rabins, author of *Divinity School*, composer of *Girls In Trouble*

Walking Triptychs
by Ilya Gutner

These are poems from when I walked about Shanghai and thought about the meaning of the Holocaust.

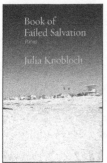

Book of Failed Salvation
by Julia Knobloch

"These beautiful poems express a tender longing for spiritual, physical, and emotional connection. They detail a life in movement—across distances, faith, love, and doubt."
—David Caplan, author, *Into My Garden*

Daily Blessings: Poems on Tractate Berakhot
by Hillel Broder

"Hillel Broder does not just write poetry about the Talmud; he also draws out the Talmud's poetry, finding lyricism amidst legality and re-setting the Talmud's rich images like precious gems in end-stopped lines of verse."
—Ilana Kurshan, author of *If All the Seas Were Ink*

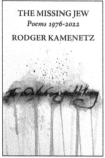

The Missing Jew: Poems 1976-2022
by Rodger Kamenetz

"How does Rodger Kamenetz manage to have so singular a voice and at the same time precisely encapsulate the world view of an entire generation (also mine) of text-hungry American Jews born in the middle of the twentieth century?"
—Jacqueline Osherow, author, *Ultimatum from Paradise* and *My Lookalike at the Krishna Temple: Poems*

The Red Door: A dark fairy tale told in poems
by Shawn Harris

"THE RED DOOR, like its poet author Shawn C. Harris, transcends genres and identities. It is an exploration in crossing worlds. It brings together poetry and story telling, imagery and life events, spirit and body, the real and the fantastic, Jewish past and Jewish present, to spin one tale."
—Einat Wilf, author, *The War of Return*

The Matter of Families
by Robert Deluty

"Robert Deluty's career-spanning collection of New and Selected poems captures the essence of his work: the power of love, joy, and connection, all tied together with the poet's glorious sense of humor. This book is Deluty's masterpiece."
—Richard M. Berlin, M.D., author of *Freud on My Couch*

CPSIA information can be obtained
at www.ICGtesting.com
Printed in the USA
LVHW010239260722
724372LV00005B/239

9 781953 829306